POLAR ANIMALS
LIFE IN THE FREEZER

WALRUSES

by Ruth Owen

WINDMILL
BOOKS ™

New York

Published in 2013 by Windmill Books, An Imprint of Rosen Publishing
29 East 21st Street, New York, NY 10010

Produced for Windmill by Ruby Tuesday Books Ltd
Editor for Ruby Tuesday Books Ltd: Mark J. Sachner
US Editor: Sara Antill
Designer: Emma Randall
Consultant: Joel Garlich-Miller, USFWS, Marine Mammals Management, Anchorage, Alaska

Photo Credits:
Cover, 1, 4, 8–9, 9 (top), 11, 12–13, 16–17, 19, 28–29 © Shutterstock; 5, 7, 20–21, 23, 24–25, 26–27 © FLPA; 15 © Wikipedia Creative Commons (public domain); 29 (top) © istockphoto.

Library of Congress Cataloging-in-Publication Data

Owen, Ruth, 1967–
Walruses / by Ruth Owen.
    p. cm. — (Polar animals: life in the freezer)
Includes index.
ISBN 978-1-4777-0220-8 (library binding) — ISBN 978-1-4777-0227-7 (pbk.) —
ISBN 978-1-4777-0228-4 (6-pack)
1. Walrus—Juvenile literature. I. Title.
QL737.P62O94 2013
599.79'9—dc23
                                    2012025846

Manufactured in the United States of America

CPSIA Compliance Information: Batch # BW13WM: For Further Information contact Windmill Books, New York, New York at 1-866-478-0556

CONTENTS

A GIANT FROM THE DEEP

Deep in the icy-cold ocean waters off the coast of Alaska, a huge animal has been feeding. Now, it swims up to the water's surface. Two giant, white **tusks** suddenly appear from underwater. Is it some kind of mythical sea monster?

No! It's a huge bull walrus. Weighing as much as a rhinoceros, the animal hooks its tusks into some floating ice and uses them to drag its massive body from the water.

Walruses are large marine **mammals**. They are members of the animal group called **pinnipeds**. This group includes seals, sea lions, and elephant seals. Walruses spend about two-thirds of their lives in the ocean. When on ice or land, they move clumsily. In the water, however, these excellent swimmers move easily and can reach speeds of over 20 miles per hour (32 km/h).

Pinnipeds

Seal

Sea lion

Elephant seal

THE WORLD OF THE WALRUS

Walruses live in freezing ocean waters in the **Arctic** region.

There are two types of walruses—Pacific walruses and Atlantic walruses. Pacific walruses live in the Bering, Chuckchi, and Laptev Seas, close to the coasts of Alaska and Russia. Atlantic walruses live in the ocean off the coasts of Greenland and Canada.

Walruses live in areas where there are ice shelves and ice floes. Ice shelves are vast floating sheets of ice that are still attached to land. Ice floes are large chunks of free-floating ice. Walruses need this floating ice as a place to rest when they leave the water.

WHERE WALRUSES LIVE

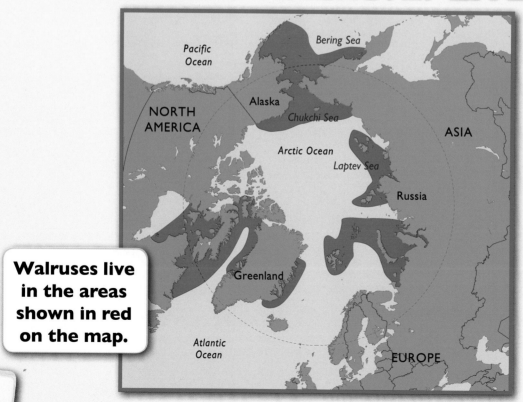

Walruses live in the areas shown in red on the map.

These walruses are resting on an ice floe.

There are around 250,000 walruses living in the Arctic.

PHYSICAL FACTS

Walruses have large bodies. Males can grow up to 12 feet (3.7 m) long. Females are smaller, but some still grow to be 10 feet (3 m) long.

A large bull walrus can be as heavy as 3,700 pounds (1,678 kg), while a female can weigh up to 1,200 pounds (544 kg).

Walruses have pocket-like body parts inside their throats that they can fill with air. Just like a swimmer wearing a rubber tube or armbands, these air-filled pockets help a walrus float in anupright position. Sometimes they even sleep while floating upright in the water!

Adult male walrus

Front flippers

Walruses have pinkish-brown skin that can be 1.5 inches (4 cm) thick. Their skin has many wrinkles and folds and is covered in a layer of short, rough hairs. Male walruses grow lumps, known as "bosses," on their necks and shoulders.

On land, walruses use their two front flippers a little like legs for walking. In the ocean, they steer with their front flippers and use their back flippers to propel their bodies through the water.

Skin lumps, or "bosses"

Wrinkled skin

Back flipper

SURVIVING LIFE IN THE FREEZER

Walruses spend a large part of their lives in water with temperatures below freezing. So how do their bodies withstand the icy cold?

Walruses are very well insulated. Under their skin they have a thick layer of fat, called blubber, which keeps them warm. This blubber can be nearly 4 inches (10 cm) thick, and can make up one-third of a walrus's body weight.

Another way in which a walrus's body stays warm is by conserving the heat in its blood. When a walrus enters the water, its **blood vessels** move blood away from the skin so that heat in the blood isn't lost. This can make a walrus that has been in the cold water for a long time look white. When the animal is back on land being warmed by the air or Sun, the blood returns to the skin's surface, and the skin gets its color back.

A walrus's flippers are rough on the bottoms to help the animal grip onto slippery ice and snow.

Good insulation and conservation of blood heat keep walruses warm in freezing water.

TUSKS

Both male and female walruses grow tusks, although the males' are much longer and heavier. Walrus tusks are made from **ivory** and are canine teeth that have grown to be super-long.

Walruses use their tusks to help pull their huge bodies out onto floating ice when they want to leave the water. Sometimes they simply hook their tusks into some ice to hold their heads out of the water while they rest or sleep with their bodies still in the ocean.

When a walrus is swimming under a large sheet of floating ice, it can use its tusks to break through the ice to make a breathing hole.

During the **mating** season, male walruses often fight over females. A male will use his tusks to jab at a rival's neck and shoulders during a fight.

Female walruses have shorter tusks than males.

An adult male walrus's tusks can grow to be 3 feet (0.9 m) long. Each tusk can weigh up to 12 pounds (5.4 kg).

A walrus's tusks are extra-long teeth.

WALRUS WHISKERS

A walrus has stiff whiskers, or bristles, above its mouth. These whiskers, called **vibrissae**, are a kind of mustache. Growing in up to 15 rows, a walrus's mustache may have as many as 700 bristles!

These walrus whiskers aren't normal hairs, however. Each bristle contains blood and nerves and is very sensitive.

Walruses use their vibrissae to find **prey**, such as shellfish and other ocean animals, on the seabed. To hunt for food, a walrus swims along the seabed squirting water out of its nostrils. The blasts of water stir up the sand and stones revealing animals that are buried on the seabed. The walrus then uses its sensitive whiskers to feel for any movements from its prey.

Nostrils

A walrus's vibrissae can grow to be 1 foot (30 cm) long. They usually get worn down, however, when the animal is using them to search for food.

Vibrissae

WHAT'S ON THE MENU?

Walruses usually **forage** for food on the seabed in water that is no deeper than 160 feet (50 m). They stay underwater for up to 10 minutes at a time on each foraging dive.

Walruses hunt for clams, mussels, crabs, snails, and worms. They sometimes eat **echinoderms**, such as starfish and sea urchins.

Soft-bodied animals, such as starfish, are swallowed whole. To remove animals with shells, such as clams, from their hard covering, a walrus will hold the animal in its lips and then suck the creature out of its shell. A walrus's suction power is so strong that walruses in zoos have been known to remove paint from the walls of their enclosures by sucking on it!

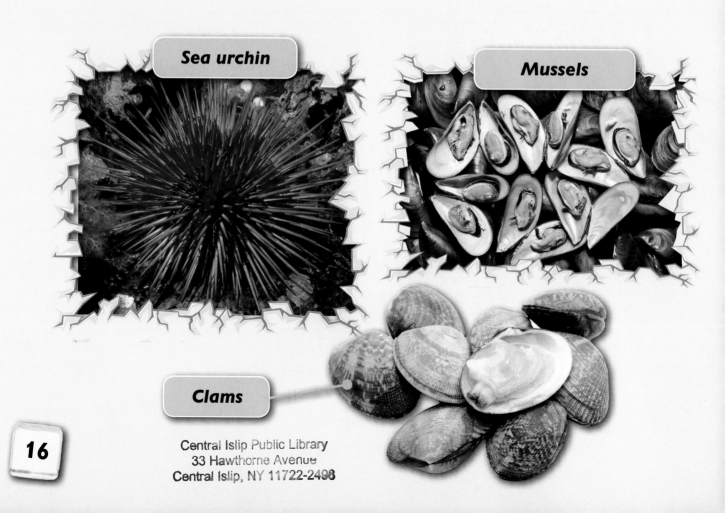

Sea urchin

Mussels

Clams

An adult walrus can eat a huge quantity of food in a day. In fact, it may eat up to 6,000 clams in just one meal!

ROOM FOR ONE MORE?

When walruses are not in the water, they rest on ice or land. This is known as hauling out. Sometimes thousands of walruses may haul out in one place!

With their huge, heavy bodies and spiky tusks, it might seem that walruses would be more comfortable with a little personal space around them. However, these animals prefer to rest with their neighbors, touching on all sides in a mass of blubber and tusks!

The biggest, most **dominant** animals get the best resting places within a crowd. If a large walrus wants the spot where a smaller animal is lying, it throws back its head and points its tusks at the smaller walrus. If this display doesn't convince the smaller animal to give up its place, it may then receive a nasty blow from the tusks of the more dominant animal.

During the mating season, male and female walruses spend time together. At other times, however, females usually haul out in all-female herds with their young, and males haul out in male-only herds.

THE BATTLE FOR FEMALES

In the walrus mating season, females gather on the ice in herds of around 20 animals. Then, it's time for the males to win them by showing off their singing skills!

Two males will float in the ocean close to an ice floe where a female herd is waiting to be entertained. The males perform by clucking, whistling, and clacking their teeth together. Underwater, they make clicking noises and sounds like bells ringing.

Two male walruses fighting over females

If a female is impressed by a male's performance, she leaves the ice and mates with him in the ocean.

Sometimes putting on a good show isn't enough, however. Then a male may need to fight another male in tusk-to-tusk combat. This will show the female audience who is the strongest, most dominant bull, and the best father for their young.

Female walruses begin to mate when they are six to 10 years old. Young males do not begin to mate until they are about 15 years old and are large enough and dominant enough to impress females.

WAITING FOR BABY

Walruses mate in winter, in January or February. The females do not give birth, however, until spring the following year. That's about 16 months later!

For the first four or five months of a female walrus's pregnancy, the baby does not grow or develop. Then, in around June or July, it begins to grow.

After another 10 to 11 months, the baby, or calf, is ready to be born in spring. This long pregnancy ensures that a calf's birth and first few months of life happen during spring and summer when the Arctic weather is less harsh.

When a female is ready to have her baby, she moves away from other females and gives birth to a single calf on an ice floe.

A walrus calf can swim as soon as it is born.

A female walrus underwater

MOTHERS AND CALVES

Female walruses with calves get together in nursery herds with other mothers and their babies. They are very protective of their calves and form strong **bonds** with them. Male walruses do not help care for their young.

A walrus calf drinks milk from its mother's body. This **nutritious** food helps the calf gain up to 2 pounds (0.9 kg) of weight each day. Its body can also grow up to 6 inches (15 cm) in length every month. As the calf gets older, it sometimes eats adult food, but it may continue to feed on milk from its mother until it is two years old.

Mother walrus

Female calves may continue living with their mothers when they reach adulthood. Male calves leave their mothers and join a male herd when they are two to three years old.

A newborn walrus calf is around 3 to 4 feet (0.9–1.2 m) long and can weigh up to 165 pounds (75 kg).

Walrus calf

DANGEROUS TIMES

Unlike their seal cousins, walruses cannot spend weeks or months in the ocean. They need to regularly rest and leave the water. But what happens if there is not enough ice for them to haul out onto?

Warmer temperatures caused by **climate change** mean that in summer there is now less ice floating in the ocean in the Arctic. With no ice to rest on, walruses have to come onto beaches and thousands are forced to haul out

In times when there was plenty of sea ice to dive from, walruses would forage for food in many different parts of the ocean. Scientists are worried that if thousands of walruses are forced to gather on one beach, there will not be enough food for them all in the surrounding ocean.

in the same few places. In fact, scientists have witnessed up to 40,000 walruses hauled out in just one area!

This change in the walruses' behavior has led to a very dangerous situation for the animals. When thousands of walruses are resting on a beach and become frightened by a polar bear, humans, or noises from aircraft, they panic. Then thousands of animals try to **stampede** back into the safety of the ocean at once. On beaches where this has happened, smaller walruses, especially calves, have been crushed to death in the stampede.

A herd of walruses stampeding into the ocean

HUMANS AND WALRUSES

Walruses and humans have a long history. For thousands of years, walruses have been an important source of meat and other materials for native Alaskans.

In the 1800s, hunters from other parts of the world killed walruses for their blubber, which could be boiled to make oil. Today, only native Alaskans are allowed to hunt walruses and the hunters may only kill enough animals to supply their food needs.

If a walrus is being stalked today, the hunter may be a scientist about to shoot a satellite transmitter into the animal's blubber. With climate change threatening the walruses' home, scientists are tracking walruses using

satellites to find out where they go and where they haul out. This will help scientists find out how changes to the Arctic sea ice are affecting walruses.

There may be difficult times ahead for these polar animals that were designed by nature for life in the freezer. Let's hope it's not too late to save their icy Arctic world!

An Eskimo dagger made from walrus tusk ivory

Native hunters used every part of a walrus. Its skin was used to make kayaks, its intestines could be made into waterproof clothing, and its stomach made a useful container. A walrus's tusks could be carved into tools or craft items. Native Alaskans still make craft items from walrus ivory today.

GLOSSARY

Arctic (ARK-tik)
The northernmost area on Earth, which includes northern parts of Europe, Asia, and North America, the Arctic Ocean, the polar ice cap, and the North Pole.

blood vessel
(BLUD VEH-sul)
A tube, such as a vein or artery, that carries blood around a body.

bond (BOND)
An extremely strong connection.

climate change
(KLY-mut CHAYNJ)
The slow warming of planet Earth. Climate change is happening because gases from burning fuels such as coal and oil gather high above the planet and trap the Sun's heat.

dominant (DAH-mih-nent)
Strongest and most powerful.

echinoderm
(ih-KY-nuh-derm)
Spiny-skinned animals with no backbones that live on the seabed. They usually have five arms, or body parts, that radiate from a central point.

forage (FOR-ij)
To move from place to place looking for food.

ivory (EYEV-ree)
A hard, white material. The tusks of elephants and walruses are made of ivory.

mammal (MA-mul)
A warm-blooded animal that has a backbone and usually has hair, breathes air, and feeds milk to its young.

mating (MAYT-ing)
Coming together in order
to have young.

nutritious (noo-TRIH-shus)
Containing nutrients, such as
vitamins, that a body needs to
help it live and grow.

pinniped (PIH-nuh-ped)
One of a group of mammals
that includes seals, sea lions,
and walruses. Pinnipeds have
flippers and spend a lot of
time in the ocean.

prey (PRAY)
An animal that is hunted by
another animal as food.

stampede (stam-PEED)
A sudden mass movement
of animals, usually due to
fear or panic.

tusk (TUSK)
A long, pointed tooth that
grows outside of the mouth.

vibrissae (vy-BRIH-see)
Sensitive bristles, or
whiskers, on the face of a
walrus that the animal uses
for detecting prey.

Websites

For web resources related to the subject of this book, go to:
www.windmillbooks.com/weblinks and select this book's title.

READ MORE

King, Zelda. *Walruses*. Marine Mammals. New York: PowerKids Press, 2012.

Rustad, Martha E. H. *Walruses*. Ocean Life. Mankato, MN: Capstone Press, 2006.

Weber, Valerie J. *Walruses*. Animals That Live in the Ocean. New York: Gareth Stevens, 2009.

INDEX